TIME SERVED
&
ALWAYS THERE

Two Collections of Poetry

By Russell Buker

Published by Piscataqua Press
An imprint of RiverRun Bookstore
142 Fleet Street Portsmouth, NH 03801
www.riverrunbookstore.com
www.piscataquapress.com

Printed in the United States of America

ISBN: 978-1-944393-26-7

1. Time Served

by

Russell Buker

For my grandsons

Foreword

The black Ducks and rock grey Doves peck through my fireplace ashes and I am reminded that my pre- Neanderthal ancestors used to do the same with clumps of dung from huge herbivores in an attempt to stave off hunger by gleaning undigested seeds along with remnants of psilocybin mushrooms that brought on primitive stages of conscious as part of their minds seemed to separate from their bodies. Shamanic prophesies soon followed until their body and the body of earth became a necessary focus by using language other than that of danger.

Now I having reached an age when too many friends are counting their last gasps in an effort to celebrate and to savor them. Which leads me to think that I may have stumbled onto the meaning of poetry, my own poetry at least, as everyone focuses on a simple, and therefore usually taken for granted, as their own breathing. Basho warned and said of himself that ever since his windswept spirit began to write poetry it never felt peace with itself but was prey to all sorts of doubts because poets work more or less blindly, run by a sensibility hidden deep inside and buffeted constantly, especially in my case, by having only a smallish number of readers which, all in all, should be less reason for one to continue writing. Why bother if not a single line will remain in the readers mind for a nanosecond past the poets demise. Well, maybe, but I continue to self publish in the wild rationalization that posterity, beautiful posterity's winds will befriend and uncover these samples.

Corvid

fabulous blue-
jay
zoot-suited

blue
on grey-white,
big

shouldered bluffs
and
spiked hair-do

with Kamakazie dives,
full
gular traveling bags

Ravens and white caps

always make me
wonder
if I will still
be
a writer when I
hit
the other side
or
if my audience'll
change
the way I have to
sing-
newer beginnings,
groan,
using only silent
consonants
that barely had asper-
ations,
thoughts in this dense
air
but have a clarity,
emotion
in such clear-shine
contract-
ing in dark matter's
grip

Shaking ever so gently

I did not know where I
was:
somewhere along the
way
getting tired with the
partial
moon's one eye, sad
eye,
lying above an old, stone
wall
all the time gravitational
waves
wanting anonymity of
anonymous
ripples whose space-time
fame
burns through simple grave
stones
of poet's exploding stars,

merging
black holes laid to rest
in
new sounds, real or
imagined,
sounds of pain setting

chains of burden in so
many
others- Scorpio drawn to
Orion-

and all you will ever
get:
small patches of blue,
cloud
or inkling of light over
shaken
headstone, perhaps, a back-

hoe
digging around to deposit
tanks
for gasoline with your
many
positions of sleep

The ultimate ordinary

I would love to travel
the speed
of light in a dark, still
night

not knowing where to
go,
stop, or come back. Who
would

spread a hand on my back
for warmth
once the impulse has gone
without

relatives without anything
to do
but hurry on unheard, not
hearing

gone really but still bright
near
you until I pass through you,
going

Askance

no explanations
for
my inherited silent speech:
how
many bodies were,
are
there in my saturated
shoe's
strange gilt- beings in
easy
sediment's gift of
where
I've been, contracting
now
in warming sun that
explains
everything to me
again
as I am warned to
take
shoes off at the door

Strain

the wind is flying all
around
while lake ice is making
up
from both our shores

in
medias res, I wait like
lake's
middle for the unheard
words

that so far huddle
under
wind-slap's rioting, I'm
just
lying in cold contem-

plation
unable to feel for now any
reason
I had allowed my ice's
last

departure, wind-crazy
journey
to the dam, a mere slip
of
the tongue away

Philos

you know, I hope,
that it is impossible
to get anywhere
following something
in this clear sky

yet you insist on
becoming a long, thin
filament of night light
not always bright

more like the accidental
light that suddenly
blew into somnolent
dark matter of our

shocked universe's
talon, tight darkness
now everyone arcs
rightward while we
travel in semi-circles

Jen ne Sais quoi

Engineered without
maps
and yet there I go again
words
and papyrus' different
engine
with cells aligned, giddy
in
their own conversations

these dull days expire
early
gasping in moving, livid
fog-
jungled stone-works of
Misiones
that have struggled
fore-
ever to tell lies, false
suppositions,
tears of deceitful, hysterical
stones

thirsting seasonally I have
thrown
myself away again
always
fire-saled whatever was
me

11

produced by so many
sleep-
less dreams that have by
now
died in the long third
quarter,
in wordless replays, sight-
less
attics hiding in their elegant
prison

The shot

came while I
grew
at my desk

computer humming
its
slow throb into my

distance, then the
silence
listening for a thud,

footsteps retreating,
animal
scream of dissolution

instead my lungs
pain
without oxygen

how does one
live
in such silence

thank god I was not
brave
foot soldier calmed

even without thud
nor
footsteps retreating

or cordite smell
splash
on my shingles

yes I live to fight
another
day at my desk

Why

it seems very
long
ago, way before
You
arrived here that
I
had climbed to the
top
of Mount Everest
taking
pictures up above
my
head to see, if I
could,
where I had come
from

When I returned to
base
people milled around
asking
if I had taken any
pictures:
well the top was too
cloudy
today and all I saw
departed

I will

never forget that
look in their eyes

when the rough,
snow-filled wind

stopped momentarily
and the finches

came to the feeder
and all attempted

to gain the chosen
feeding hole, one

of nine, or the next
time they arrived

another hole was
chosen and as I

watch from my
window can only

wonder who among
them chooses those

various holes. So
for dinner with the

treachery of an old
man that night I set

one plate in the tables
middle with food.

dumbfounded at first
my children soon, to

soon, dispensed with
utensils and chose

whatever pleased them.
certainly the table got

a little messy and I was
amazed how quickly

they filled up then left
the table with its clean

napkins without anyone
asking to be excused

March madness

or standing on what I
hope
to be the edge

March icicles again,
roads
blown closed,
pictures out the
picture
window are void
on
the bottom and
I
am compacted in
snow
readied for shipping-
thought
you were going too-
oh
those are all grown
the way a stream
encircles
my boot and keeping
watchful
eye as this season's
love

has been far away, a small
echo,
tonic chord, has been
tugging
my ears for some time
now
Wonder how long,
lost
my purpose in them
and
only became aware
lately
to the land of unfurl,
springing
slow furl where the
heated
sun damages our
thinking
leading us on in cruel
wealth
of perfect water to the
sea

Stoic

I've never been as
stoic
waiting on the plow
to clear
my car immobilized in
the lane

I watch this night's
snow
with its steely, cold
fractal
tentacles that have
joined

themselves into un-
imaginable
shapes that patiently
wait
the wispy demise of
everything

architectural, nocturnally
gained,
knowing the tug of water
has
even on the frozen
mountain

tops has been carefully
collecting
dust for clouds and wind
buoyed
in evaporation's mist
with

no idea where it will
land
but now I hear the plow
and
at least part of me will
escape

R

I was always alone with
all the gods
of antiquity as I held my
dead dogs
in my arms at that moment
what happened to Ricky
invoked
each time one left me

there were no fangs just
a smile when
my first that we all loved
we were
so young to know how
repetitive
this would become as
he stood

in line for his spoon of
cod liver,
ate our leftover food to
release us
from the dinner table,
who had
no speeding dump trucks
shiny moon

hubcaps, who now was still,
sleeping mode,
unlike dogs I had seen die
before
legs trying to run away
from their
pain, snapping at what hurt
so inside
or whining eyes imploring
our administer
extending legs out in stiff
good by

no Ricky just laid there as
I picked
him up in his silence as my
silent tears
drafted down on him and our
long fears
of remembrance both sleeping on
my bed

Rental

we rented walls of
wood
and glass, gladly lived
out-
side most days, came
in-
side when night ruined
our
vision, cold massaged
our
backs and in the winter
watched
through our epiphragn
cold
overtake everything
then
close it in with blankets
of
snow and as we watched
felt
ourselves go slower,
stayed
up nights to hurry the
season
and could live again out-
side
in the brittle unrest of
opening
sliding glass doors

Corpus

It is not as
though
we will have
to
come from another
planet

this micro chip,
our
new earth, is
so
flat and linear it
invites

you in, a video
smear.
Your callosum
divided
brain that you were
allowed

will now become a
sound
and picture bite
of

you and may even
give

you
your new name

WS

access is the first
part of perception

even if the access
is through someone else's

eyes or mouth or gesture
or steel-toed boot-

wonderful emphasizer
that it is, can be-

just a lot of moon
light does not make

up for lack of light as
the polyurethanes veneer

of civilization's mighty
thin, biting and kicking

each other at the Font
of Monsanto, Nestlé's urge

or the heavy sea is itself
a song that encompasses

other songs, loudly swallowed
in compact's, contract   with

perceptions vocal permanence
of images briefly held by sand

Dear

we purple older
chapter two
is way down
the road

third eye
pineal glands
can not see out,
watching

me crumble
with the sick apple
I took to sea.
racked with inflated

pain which held my
joints together,
ripeness is allowing
day dreams of

a thin, dark narcotic
that flows over,
understanding
solitude through

through these bones
harsh rain continuing
or tidal black light
that finally flows

full reaching shores
top where I can roll
with silent logs
of springing tide

caressed in rock
weeds pliant fingers
before the grating door
of emptying water

Puerta

where are my edges,
strictures, ness/less I
crammed in overhead

bins before the numb-
ness flying around so
loosely brings

This year our under
standing of April
will be different

our bewilderment will
quietly lessen
from a stern March:

ice on our wings, roofs,
seat belts clicked through
take-off, exit signs off

I feel myself a misplaced
hinge on the cabin side
of the aisle curtain

with twenty per-centers
all back-lit with cold
regrets in their dark

who among us has brought
up a memo as to where we
are heading, when and if

we will arrive, shifting
in our seats, whether
the dark is more sacred

than the light or if blue
angels will continue to
proffer hands on shoulders

Recon

Soon this spring's
dark diamonds

slowly settle in.
welcoming lake

accepts all
memories tricks,

also aqueous, to
drown in chaotic

kinship decoded
in the wealth of

delinquent fears
darkness brings

with hopeless screams
on disturbed silt

and unremembered
wise whys or how's

this regeneration thing's
going to work out

Snow Belle

southern arrested
with the soft hands

of early flowers
strangled in aromatic

delightful tongue
while we await

the long goodbye with
stiffened joints in

tundra's slow drying
as the snow on the

ground left yesterday
without waving any

promises leaving us
lodged between

remembering yester-
days who are you,

where are you
on the barrenness

of this early spring's
long-legged daylight

tricking all to straighten
seeking snapshot's awe

no matter the distance
or imagined   aroma

Remember

night:
a distant bird in the
tree
cries out in my dark-
ness,
waking wind worried,
or
wanting conversation
not
with you but another
avian
god to settle its sanct-
uary.
why not me? I
cackle
knowing too well
that
I am unseen and
supposedly
know nothing at all
about
black night's wind-
fingers
my circle of friends
remember,
to close their eyes,
wake
with the sun

Glean

shadows
listen as people
sleep

where
there is no garbage
to sift

on
moon-rubbed
ground

on
empty plastic
bags

dream
tomorrow's trucks
afford

better
being before they
pass

in
silence's final
collection

no
comment between
drivers
wishing

he had and glad he
had

not
commented or
thanked

gleaners
for keeping the pile
down

Two

I owe one
life
to those shapes

in
trees, some real
flying

down for food,
some
unreal and it is to

those
who were not real
that

I owe the most
for
I have had to

explain
myself, my fears
because

able to imagine
all
sorts of song-colors,

behaviors
and happenings in
life

extrapolated into
prayers
for everyone with-

out
markers or collective
plot's

remarkable mix
just
starting over again

Clouds

my skiff sits still,
clouds are moving
silently,
wind gathers strength
across my bow, across
dimensions
of blues and greens,
waves swell bumping
me
up and down while sweet
music calls the whiteness,
souls,
from fish below to graze
granite headstones where
unblocked,
salmonid, ancestors strain
to peek at their duende
heaven
of supple trees, billowing
grasses bowing casually to
earth;
my half-full skiff wallows,
plows horizontally to waves
mercy:
someone in the same boat
waves frantically with his

single
oar but can not hear my
wind returned helpful
prayer

The words

I take with me are an
enormous
pile that would not
protest
more, love more
than
those I printed on
impending
darkness   and you
were not
simply discarded, clink-
piled
awkwardly in a forgotten
room
somewhere in my mind
where
you will always follow-
always
follow me: gaunt, silent
wolves
with blue, staring eyes

Talk less

black mounds
surround   your

gauze powdered
face, grave and

inert, joyless
in exile on this

Memorial Day
and C.elegans

thanks indeed
verso, recto of

rough woman
twisting away

what century
is your confusion

history with
out function

other than
excretion

of bacteria
and 300 self

inseminated
larvae begin

to chew their
way through

swinging doors
that admit no

light past the
soulful diaphragm,

air pocket,
surrounding what

was once my
robust father's

second escape
air pistoned

past his chiseled,
chosen stone

Note to Patrick
Werifesteria

Take your time
son
lets not race
apart

I will take my
gum,
my dad-gum
too

blanker than the
wet,
starless night
spent

beside a quiet
lake
wondering was
I

asleep with an
orange
bird hovering,
flying

among blue spring
moths
listening to their
songs,

the prettiest victims
one
ever could see or
hear

Grateful

Gratefully
standing on the moon:
dream
is possible !. What
next
the impossible
dream

Now and again

Yesterday we were not home
it was raining hard and
a small box had been left
in the shed by the delivery man

Already spiders had claimed
it as their hunting territory. Well,
well, I thought, those books had
better beware coming out

again cocooned in time's
cherished tastefulness, in its
sticky grasp heightening
their supposed worth

It was another joke in my life
here, my exes   and mine,
well rationalized   with the
perforations surrounding

the non-forever stamp of it
all denoting time, location
and day it was sent to
those wispy, sticky spiders

All those

of all those writers
you're constantly
reading, talking to

I'll bet you are the
only one with BBQ
sauce on your shirt-

front and yet for once
I hesitate to give up
this shirt to wash

for once the feel is
distinctive even though
no one else notices
except the new puppy

that focuses entirely
on my single, allowed
glass of beer dribbling
down its tongue

Guilty as hell

I am the one who has self
indulged in 16 books by
as-in-mine press left to molders
in rotting landscapes

where one can only see
from where one is standing
foliage of an uncaring sea
of thought deemed real

our president has no strategy,
no none, only a bowl of Wheaties,
heroes crawl our Spartan stage
sugared with industrial milk

that tells me you came too late
mi amore- did I say that right-?
I've got to learn to translate
another you, bed and table

for when we fall from varying
lengths true dark: makes an unseen
glow, makes one snuggle their
shadow and imagine we are

blossoms within waters slow
and forceful flow back to the
dirty air of profit with cool,
hazy sunlight and half a shadow

Birch

It is war-like in this
grove,
still unable to read those
signs;
lost myself for the last time
walking
among these Birch trees: ghost
oceans,

unbidden shadows move
through
this darkness' wide water
where
the silences and twigs break
with
a revolvers clarity, moaning
red

there are so many here groaning
up
a hateful seashore, clinging to
ankles,
my ankles, in this daylight
dark
fear of a white-legged tick's
alien
hollow point's shatter unhewed
mood

Washing

the roots of radishes
some-
how makes me wonder
how
widely we missed the
mark
as if the only goal to
follow
that strange urge, not
necessarily
geotropic, that never
presented
itself as a bull's eye
or
spot of red laser but
followed
the soil we were in
before
memory dimmed and
some-
thing hauled you out
though
you had not a flower
nor
fruit to speak of but
out

you came with only the
slight
hope that the slicing knife
stays
sharp for there is no
TIP
to give whomever

open

I open
nothing by chance

the cat
and I, unpinned,

move
window to window

docked
and domesticated

only
ease and a favorite

chair
without leaving

a mark
maybe a smallish

streak
in the liquidity

of
Cyber Space

beyond
flat paned glass

Times

between our talking
to each
other in sleep and
when
awake shows how
little
we understand here

as the talk turns to
how
we both handle our
hamburgers
sliding out of the bun
while
attempting to eat slowly

or where we would
go
if we could afford to.
then
how we would call
to
each other nightly

saying this is not what
I
expected but. do you like
where
you went or should we
have
stayed home talking more

between sleep's awake
and choices we make

Wind

Can not believe how
many green leaves were
sacrificed today in

this wind that has in-
directly pollinated
us: we are field and

flowers, surrounding
trees, shrubs whether
we stand tall or lie

down in the fine ferment
of fog, of an early spring
morning's full swing, a dawn.

welcoming airborne insects
and the invisible, hair raising,
body-covering breeze

we have become one
holding our fern-fertile
hands as enough reason

to walk so far into
the beginning sunlight
oblivious to stinging

The last fire

I was left handed,
strange,

they left me with
the children

making spears, now
my knees

are still supple and I,
ultimate,

go with them, throw the
first spear,

they love me and
take turns

watching the children,
feeding

the fires within stone
stars,

coarse petals sublime
sleep

at my feet, a hand on
my arm

she comes to me,
she

comes to, to ME!
strange

Am

I thawing Plutonian dotted
equator
or someone in trouble
singing

taking most fascicles
with you
from Cetus' borrowed
atmosphere

you wait for me to
accept
all of your different
beings,

heritage notifications,
yet
even though they do
not

pertain to me what
am
I to become: a tremendous
mistake,

life-like, breathless in my
solitary,
quiet, tiny-self again
terminally

timed in this slow rush
of
your going away
again

Waiver

Sappho, her moon seeming
hair
was down for me, she laughed
at my
ungainly attempt on the
trembling
apple on her tense, flowing
bough
Give, yes give up this
foolishness

this is this and
that
is whitened that

you seem
to waver not only
from
joint cartilage ground
between
the bones or memories
tricks
splotched in frost's grip
and yes,
have shown a fear

in all
your bones that all
your
thoughts were down-
right
worthless and if you
recognize
one more sun know
your
life is one of constant

waver
of voice and gait and
best
keep a head bowed
self
out of everyone's way
till all
the coin tosses of
sun
and moon are spent

Floral

Fearful, grown too old,
teary,
to enjoy watching
all

those colored Petunia
heads
you piled on grey, fire-
place

ashes where they
remain
silent thoughts, their
wilt

girding themselves
with
dark dreams flighty
conduit,

shimmering, for wintering
bees
grooming themselves in
hives

Requiem
Kenneth Allen

The ashes finally are
home
we search dwindling
supply
of appropriate
cards

cards that will never
know
our hope that the un-
drownable
demons are gone or
quiet

in grey resting place
among
family's hope for peace,
god-
speed and love for you
always

This

is it, once again
between
breaths you wonder

if our path through
will
prove whether running
or

walking will allow
our
gaunt frames to be the
drier

when this storm's
done
attempting dampening
spirits

in the soggy sway of
moving
on once again, once
again

Where

Gone, where, you'd think.
lost
when I refuse to press,
again,
my forehead on your
back-
lit screen, allow my
eyes
a drizzle through squalid,
arid
vowels, deformed consonants
thoughts
your mind will entertain

where
the trail through those
words,
a mere ten minutes from
home,
whose godless signs are still
wrong-
while we circle-walk losing
energy
to focus through gravity's
center,
lightening feet, cloudy
sand

Lost and found

This is certainly the
best
group that I have been
with
in a long time and yet
lost
again unable to take
comfort
in the web of dew on
the grass

Seems there is still a
calling
of names I gave my
hurts,
groans of history and
short
order cooks as warming
leaves
watch while thoughts
are

dismantled in the light
through
Pine needles' sharpened
points
to a steady white blare
where
everything becomes un-

seen
especially those traveling
with

70

There

if my art of loneliness,
being
alone, is landscape then
I'm
lost there where my eyes
enjoy
memorable light or its
lack

used to tell my
players
don't look down! The
floor
is flat and the ball is
round
it will seek your hand
out

Now I'm not so darn
sure
cause logics inverted
you
must seek out that
ball
but don't look up
gravities

have hooked all your
balls
and you must now run
outside
on the musty lawn or its
snow
where plows or dozers
push

everything in huge piles,
fans
become worshipers, heads
bowed,
so I calmly say look
make
two passes before we
shoot

Remember

you left me prostrate and
breathing

afraid of being ever
touched

again but in making my
rooms,

tables, perfectly replace-
able

now I too want to feel
fear

in all its quick, secretive
comfort

yes, you left me,
me

remembering to breathe
between

waves as you taught me,
fine,

so damn embarrassing
being
just another copy-writer,
fine

Finally

it is quiet in the
long
hall of many key-
less

doors and that the
dog
lying there has
rationalized

all the previous merry
sounds
have been absorbed
into

bones and fur prompting
legs
and feet twitching
eliciting

quick whimpers from
one
who has seen and heard
much

Argos no longer plays
with
Encolpius' greatest
carving

in the smooth hall that
leads
to Penelope's expectant
room

where both are waiting
similar
answers to their nightly
prayers

More weight

If a stone of
equal
weight were tethered
to me
when I leave this
place,
people might think
that
that very stone was
weighted
by one so frail

yet others may
nay
to show how weighted
down
I am by this heavy
stone
or that the two of
us
deserve each other:
one
silent and one singing

forever
and as the lyrics
change
themselves their mean-
ing
remains the same for
the stone
or what I first thought
was
silent stone from some-
where

a friend, I hope, or one
who
hates me or is it the
tether
of nagging, relentless
songs
far into our dreaming
night

Neon

these are not neon
lights
here on such harsh
aridity

people slow-walking
towards
me with lengthening
shadow

these were the beauti-
ful
ones that I almost
knew

who were the hearts of
trees,
petals of flowers, grass
growing

so long ago:
breath-
less now they filter,
walk

towards me and I
want
to say to them, why
haven't

you been looking for
me,
I could awaken myself
again

and you are gone, again,
and
the crying loon will rise,
fly

Fall

my head is in the
air

freshening wind
blows

teardrops from
your

face to where
all

that was silent is
now

wet, sensing
more

in tall, dried
grass

Damp

silent, orb spider web
conjures
light coming through
a pass-
emptying from some-
where
in the door, refusing
rest
on the other side until
walled

I remember equal
lights
waking my cat also
for we
never heard the spider
working
its silken song on a
different
channel of truth than we
were on

Tropic

what is it nudges
me?
all these times I
waited
through silly vocations
till
now suddenly old
enough
to feel the strength,
feel
the real bones of
daisy
flowers with their
gold
orbed petal non-choices:
odd,
no one talks to these
weird
abstractions where our lies
choke
themselves as sunlight
breaks
dark undivided, un-
decided

September

Now can you hear
it,
the slight reverb-
eration

of everything
that
has gone full
tilt

a child on his
bike
who has done
this
\
before and now
some-
thing ahead in this
road

means he is forced
to pull
handle-bar brakes
for

the very first
time
to avoid Rubenesque
squirrels

oblivious to him
slowing,
veering back up to
speed

While

I began this
whole
thing of self,
visiting
a paupered alder
brook

you can't tell
me
as I now hustle,

careful
of tall grass,
stones,
and waiting water to
fill
my little, brook,

from
room to silent
room
to save myself

ahead
of flourishing sun
light
that I am merely
protecting
my REM's filmy

print
of hand me down
emotion

or that it will lead
me
to that wonderful
day
of judgment, Isolde's shared
paces
of blueberries, crunchy
plow

or that today I will
never
again upon waking
dream

Test drive extinction

this car is the
jam
do you feel
me

I coin a lineage
that
wants to see me
in
tights, red stockings

driving Napoleon's
unshod
horse of no color
different

in this silence of
mis-
understood jumbled
syntax

where seeking the
helper
is a worthless en-
deavor

or more than I
can
understand never
mind

feel's appropriateness'
as
jammed logic: do you
feel

Sinuous

snake that it is
my,
our Vagus nerve
runs
along a jagged
spine

opens when we're
having
the times of our
lives
closing eyes, increasing
heart

rate involuntarily to
keep
us from fainting as
our
rabbit pairs used to,
also

know that yours does
this
too and yet I do not
have
the guts to tell you
this

because I'm afraid of
what'll
happen if one or the
other
shuts down during all
this

Some

thing different
time
to leave again
Lab-
rinthitus will
tag
along for sure

I lie
down dream of
going
over the edge of
all
the chances I
took
house painting

A
friend once told
me
that if you're
not
living on the edge
you're
taking up too much
room

but
I hate not being
able
to close my
eyes
anymore with-
out
feeling I'm heading
down

to less space than I
have
ever imagined in
spite
of all my beginnings

Game Day

I chuckled to my
doctor
I have trillions of
viruses
in my virome and
don't
know good from bad

or
who is on first base,
third
and you insist on finding
my
pagan A1C, love it
below

seven as though it is
an
umpire of sorts
to
keep the ballgame
going
no matter who wins

we've all paid our
dues
no matter who slud
into
third bacteria base
they
are always a hit-

even a drag bunt
down
the first base line
of
our still being in the
game
that they decide

ebb and

remember that soft
wail
wet limestone letting
go

falling plop, into water
below
while I dismantled
steps

and then the creaking
dock
from tenuous hold on
inclined

bank as we stood knee
deep
in water that broke
against

thighs pushing every-
thing
ashore- soon I thought
I'll

be able to stand, walk
out
of here, similar to the
cave,

on osseous strings
robbed
from below, flowing
away

Warning

Listening to heavy night-rain
today did not exactly break
but still thudded down upon
fast flowing water coursing
through my yard into the lake

Rain fell all day reminding
that all my ventures, poems
were someone else's   even
from another country or may-
be strictly acid reflux all

possibly from another time
but for now the rain tool on
the light greenish hue of
someone else saying" from
me to you" just as I, wet and

confused, had to dig escape
routes diverting incessant water
flow to maintain my inert
driveway from allowing itself
to be wholly swept away

El Faro

oddly enough
I am blessed
with acute vertigo

trying to maintain
my integrity in
a patch of hallway

fortunately I'm not
top heavy
riding these dizzying
nauseous waves

and there are no trained
men and women
working about in my
creaking hold

trying to fix my
propulsion,
keeping my keel even
quietly desperate

while grateful waves
curl over
body slamming silent,
welded steel

yes I am blessed with
my vertigo
and in the dark see,
hear voices

Sensory substitution

they say that I
learned
my alphabet
lying on my back
tracing
letters on my arm's
own
data port to the brain

I heard, also, that I
learned
to drive with my
tongue
hanging out so that
later
pictures would come
if

I became tongue-tied
or
saw ghosts during
scenes
of normal distribution,
beings
in the bell curve of my
life

that suddenly started
talking
revenge from the taxi
driver,
born in the backseat
of a
Model T who quickly
learned

the addresses of every-
one
everything and the shortest
distance
to get anyone there and
parking
in the most crowded of
places

Drift

We always thought our
void
was above the lighter
horizon

not below, Melville's
white
whale gathering more
speed

from ocean depths
where
talking from one
end

of the zonal globe's
easier
in the compression of
water

long mile drenching
gutturals
unheard above, but no, we
look

up, above then reflexibly
below
not understanding that
everything

will rest on our horizon
itself
as it circles wisely the
ground

Hello

a favorite Raven is
gone

Hawk feeding on
him

while leaves slip
trees

beaming down upon
my

walk as I wish one
hello

the way he followed
game-

like wherever we went.
As

long as bones last no
elephant

is completely dead
yet

we, faint beasts that
we are,

tend to bury ourselves
under

gravel, stones, grey grave
markers

but I am grateful for these
leaves

coloring all but a simple
hello

Winter Haiku

dead stars occult
fall onto tops of grey
porous clouds
*

sinuous blockade
of green-lung respiration
wheezy weightlessness
*

half a halo
rainbow delights in hiding
x marks the spot
*

I was absent, gone
rang the rusted dinner bell
wont you stay awhile
*

dark streams reflect
most leaves have now fallen
silent winter sighs
*

another cold night
wrinkling low moon rests
thirsty waves
*

In November's

cold pink dust swirls
I am nebulous
stromatolite sensations
that stand, look
straight up in the sky

holding onto a tiny
horn of new
moon's whiteness
to allow some
vertigo play for myself

living in a comment
following Deneb with a still-
ness unfathomable
while my phone rings blue
boat-like and flooding

all tensions between my
feet and the earth
I float, floating galaxly-less
not aware that
it is all homeward

Practice being fine

Why
no one is here
holding
my hand, investing,
while

I stand on the event
horizon
back to loud birth,
balance
and anticipation

pulse
in my flight suit
that
may not be needed
after

all: where dreams of
you
vanish along with
every
day of my life:

when
this polluted lake is
still
and unbidden reflections
calmly

practice being fine
in
pinkish, lulling, morning
sun-
shine over and over

Amazing

castles down I
stumble
keep singing
while
sounds roll from
hull's
propulsion flame
toward
Innisfree water
dreams
extensive sign of
green

no musket this is
not
the time for iced
coffee,
flagging industry,
fear
of failure or the
pain
of lifting a stanza
onto
another filing voids
of space

December

the lake seemed so
quiet
for five days now
bits
of skim float errantly:
thoughts
before the big freeze

wisdom where were
you
today while a pop-
up
brown paper leaf
running
on two lobes ahead

of a relentless, red
squirrel
with its fur flying
out-
ward in the practical
oak
shivering December wind

Acute labrynthitus

With
this strange fear
I
have suddenly
known
how alive I am

vertigo burdens me
back-
pedaling from every-
thing
that seems steep

with
threats to my being too
free
of that final fall
and
does not matter for
hope
as we know it or
still
dream about nightly
with-
out fears protection

2. *Always There*

by

Russell Buker

Foreword:

Pondering the brashness of contemplating another foreword after sloughing off 16 books already with their forewordings I feel half blinded for protection while tempted to let this one go, freed from wantings, and yet I can not help but wonder if my views on writing poetry have changed all that much: well, not really, except that now I do not expect one word to dazzle the belt off of a reader so perhaps the syntax has become much looser searching for something that was always there, untouched, beneath the surface , perhaps a suspicion beyond the literal that had resisted coming to the surface without any notions of negotiation with whatever haunts us would chance , in part, who we are as we, hopefully, rescue ourselves from the jetsam and flotsam of our lives.

And of course I will have to prevail in writing no matter how much, or many, times anxiety crops up especially as I know I will have to give most books away, non-valued, which should make one feel less than coveted but by now makes me feel more adamant than ever as there is always something, always something *always there*

Terror

no need to travel
so far

diminishing energy
sputtering

here roosters do best
around

the shore picking
gleaming

sharp shards of granite,
garnets,

slanting today's sunrise
in its

many crazed versions
of

speech at the receding
dark

and crowing wattles to
their

newly acquired sun
cock-

a-doodle do to
you

Began

I don't want you to play
any-
more she wispered to me

I've grown to an anthology,
eight
more Bees will she see

as I wait and wait for
my
own penis to explode

annihilating me all to hell
after
mating with Queen Bee

and muse how so much
like
the poetry that extinguished

my own drowsy personality,
pilfering
me away to an eyeless,

non-seeing self that now will
not be
a loveable read any more

Mid point

Mere promises of
snow
after the winter's
solstice
and Celtic Candlemas
bright
trees stand in shadow's
light

in noise, burgeoning
ice,
wolves in unobtrusive
grey
fur we are, all of us,
gnawing
bleeding holes in ice
across
this expanding lake
trail

pawing nonchalantly
checking
our safety in thickness
while
eyes scan, stare hoping
to see
what exactly is going
wrong

in our back- packed
life

Oratorio

you can see me
now
that this wind and
snow
have quietly stopped

now waking in every
wildness
no longer constrained
I'm

a useful shadow, if you
will,
attempting to run
ahead

of the sun that only
measures
the time I should have
left

this is my sun with
pure,
white track of before
no

real purpose yet on the
flat
slab with my incremental
world

blanched in sunlight
for
the emphasis that is all I
have
between such storms

Salute

yes that is the right
word

upon thinking a
flower

has been deceived by
all

the warmth in this
winter

yes and once that I
have

named you you are
no

longer my god and
with-

draw to the empty blue
ether

of my, our, language
where

nothing has a name
or

meaning and where we
are

able to enjoy being
amongst

all that is or has been
or

will be in our for-
ever

ride from there to
there

Beach stone

asks my forgiveness
forgiven
interrupting a snails
stain

I was brought here
not
knowing who or what
was

going to be going
on
and yet this well pro-
tected

snail I have been a
hinderance
to her solitary walk and
now

I am truly sorry as
I
can be with all this
weight

Let's see

I have no idea what
I
say anymore: picture
words
roar past my teeth-

did I just order break-
fast
from the dinner menu
wait,
she spoke through me:

terrified
contemplating everyone
in
this restaurant, finally
told

me, again, how my words,
flinchless
metaphors, are eating
up
my world with odd

rests
still dangerous, powerful-
common,
non sequitorilarily
ritualistic

as this bare-breasted rest-
aurant
where blued men die before,
before
they finish their coffee

As

trees in the forest we
contemplate
fellow trees tipped in
storm

and they awake every
morning
to study and old, their,
face

that had been insinuated
into
their lives and it was
difficult

to see which one
suffers
the most in their *I am*
here

version of the afflicted
and
lover of the afflicted as Dr
generals

confer in md'eed, shiny
corridors
about their latest-
latest

in the sense of a new
campaign
for those in their combined
mirrors

polished every morning of
their
newly begotten lives
living

in a shrinking, older house
silent
now that the winds have
died

Bottom of the stairs

It seems as though
I'm
flying horizontal
with
the setting sun and

I feel it only fair to
warn
that there is a Raven's
picture
on my chest who if

unable to feel movement
from
my heart's center as I gain -
still-
nesses' toroidal flow, will

flap and turn, close my
eyes
and fly away down to the
river's
clever equilibrium which

will not be far enough
for
him to change one awe-
some
sun for another

Blue nights

I know how late I
am
have to dress for my
visit
with all the anxiety
you
instilled in mom's chipmunk
you,
you still so alive while
I'm
only allowed to make
infrequent
trips for visitations with
your
new trowel vibes to
smell
roses left behind on
my
last borage- borded
bed
whose blues waited
on
rose flowering well
before

you mowed them, us,
down
with more noise than
I
ever wanted to hear

Today

is Harriet's birthday
and
it rained Easterly
which
was not as much
fun

tired of searching
for
all my presense, it is
going
on three weeks with-
out
my swift glasses

there
is a stranger walking
through
my vision as though
I'm
dreaming day and night

when
he starts to walk away
I curse
him with every swear
known
to me: morphogenetic

availability, last of the
saddle
tramps, lost your
horse,
ugly, can't even stop
rain.

Stories from my brain,
do not
come back tonight, ever,
show
me your pock-marked
face

Wish

my soul that recedes
annually
a strange growing of a

thickness
in its outer ring
fit

for weathering the imo-
bilizing
salt on times silent shaft

with
no bells forlorn heard
when

the odd clank of remem-
berance
as how it was before my

birth
and I was someones
sonic,

moral rind in the din
of
living within everything

Worthy

I've never had the
pleasure
sitting with serene
monks
to argue our silent
Vortex

Lately my eyes are too
watery
for reading much at
a
time when I accepted
isolation,

negotiation and especially
not
wanting what I had so
desired
before in between the
rising,

setting of the sun
to
slip into the frigid
waters
of night where there
were

no objects to swim
towards,
hesitating only with
flashes
of inner light before
continuing

this solitary practice of
dying
leaving not a single foot-
print
before arid sunrise
dries,

dumps me on another
illogical
flowerless shoal of
speculative
rocks called, I think,
Boon Island

Night's

long, low clouds
dissipate
and on a star's
shore-
line words gather
sputtering
happily as the Worm
Moon

draws them on a
story-
line that needs re-
telling
and you can only
watch
as your old face
begins

to emerge, thicken
then
roll towards your
absent
past while the clicking
you
now hear is your
own

No walking away
now
while your tired
eyes
cast this restless beach's
words
that will fail sooner or
later

The first hinge

before my knees
went
I was strong and
balanced

now walking is
chore:
paining me at
that

I hit the sides
coming
down the long, dark
hall

swelling has re-
placed
synovial thinking:
no

longer thoughts
astral
rays of light
are

returned to my
swollen
endless memory
say

exactly what I mean,
meant
forest of words
gets

darker, quaking planck
spheres
nothing's happening
here

The Missile of feeling

Seeing to the seen
seeming poetical stasis

holding fast till
there is nothing

else to see when
mass is all about

the empathy of
geometry which

may or not be
human, fibonacci

sequence lifts the
seer from the blank

of anticipation to
guidance holding

fast till there is
nothing left to see,

memory purged of
innocent indescribable

form unable to be held
other than   pixels of

fractal groans splitting
pronoia's supported

sonic Pi in the sky of
doubt's innocent form

3:30 AM Easter

Conscious always resets
hope:
the waning moon is
hazy
but its full circle is
light
enough for me to
feed
the irruptive birds
who
have made quick
thieves
of resident Chick-a-
dees

onion bagels for
ravens
with peanuts for the
squirrels
Now with a sleeping
cat
in lap I watch blues
of
morning articulate
base
white, waiting for
another

Chickadee to land on
inky
veins bubbling this
measurable
weight- the one I
held
in my palm while he
gained
Consciousness

April 1

out of the still-
ness
of regrowth
wind

and snow bring to
mind
an earlier quiet
buried

in harsh memory
that
fills again with
snow

that will not last
tempting
icy buds to guess
again

and again what fools
us
most translating
desire

Vision

had she not looked
back
there would have
been
many pillars of
salt

everyone fleeing
does
not look forward to
un-
certain cold hearths
while

the ones they left
are
still warm, warmer,
from
the devastation of
moving

to frantic freedom
so
stopping for a while
can
not hurt really until
feet

slowly deactivate
while
crying out loud:
do not
wait up for me to-
night

Sorry

but I never knew how
to
decipher your mysteries
whom
or what you were to me

some windows were
closed
early on and some
were
watched through that glass

a
long, long time no
matter
the weather outside
I

was always aware that
you
never came inside or
looked
my eager way-ever-

recovery
is sifting sand, sudden-
ness
in walking, quick feet,
with

an ocean shore close
by
where dual footprints
stick
if we get there on time

Spent

casings lying in blood
no

wonder we turn,
burn

to violence fearing
Mercury's

frantic tumbling and
knowing

it may collide with
Venus,

restrict us to one
evening

star for poor white
birds

leaving their worn
nests

of nothingness and
prey

tell they still have
inadequate

answers, deepening fears
as

a powerful child of
one

from home, flightless
eviction

left as only remains
without

presence in a mercurial
whorl

untitled
eventuality of spent

Slap happy

it is early yet but
how

easily one wants to
rush

this part of spring
along

looking forward to
spring

blossoms in their
slow

greyness of wind and
rain

head down splash to
day

incrementally slow
rise

of screams from mute
brown

on dark brown waiting
pink

pastels of pink flowers
on

lavender's visual violence
necessary

for spring to spring's
hurtful

awakening rattle-slap,
slap,

slap of finch's purple.
gold

so loud, eyes bend, so
sharp

Gathering

this is spring again
and
I am still raking fall
leaves

that have not fallen
together,
scattered images that
my

mind must process
singly
so that my mind gets
clearer

pictures of spring's
grace,
I am unable to perceive
time's

muscle memorizing with-
out
an unconscious and my
phone

who can not reach any-
one
other than an idio-
savant

of similar processoring
worse
everything's relegated
to

the after life of voice
mail
which is probably the
only

time my being rests, when
some-
one else may account for
me

This

an awful time, yes
I
should like to be

more
guttural through these
days

it makes little sense
that
this thick ticking

away
collecting instances
of

whatever I had bor-
rowed
before landing on

this
rock where someone
tells

me there is no use
looking
any more, loomed

in
a hollow voice above
and

below fluent steps
begging
me

to follow close by
birds
as Audubon would

Maia

No one can truly
guess
how free I feel
with
the arrival of spring,

really
May, as if every-
thing
is no longer under-
ground

and
runs, flops, flashes
for
all on the prejudiced
mudl-

less landscape of this
April
whose winds seared
many
attempts of strong-

willed,
brazen flowers who
come
May may have a
distinct

shortness of breath,
gimpy
toes that do not quite
fit
their new spring shoes

All

the dreams of mine
that
have reinvented
me

from below that
dam
that seems about to
break

sunk in a serial
knowing
I could never be
adrift

trapped in this much
soap
or fossilized as an
anthology

as you will for
me
and to make matters
worse

my frame keeps cracking
while
these dreams take on
hurried

foreplay with awakening
child's
scream mowing wild
flowers

growing in our quiet
room
sufficing stroke by
stroke

Recovery

naturally the wish
was
to make it back

or
so I thought as
all

two-legged beings
walk
toward the light

old
words crammed
spinal

medullar and empty
eyes
angered at arriving

so
late in all this
rain

and ash of predawn
filling
the void filtered with

Mr
Freud, come back, yes,
bring

friends, Paracas too, who
do not
remember me at all

as
I stepped
out of Uber with but

few
words and plastic
perfect

payment card, foot
steps,
mine, wet words

sloshed

in the making light
listen

So

I see birds flying pre-
dawn
light attempting to

fly
away from their bones
in

a confused desire for
more
speed than dim hawks

you and he want to cut
my
leg off, drive a metal

spike
in it to reattach those
visions

that Mantle and I
have
to relinquish every

night- he bought a
bar
and drank every night

169

unsure
how he got home
again

I started to write poetry
so
everyone could under-

stand
bone and metal in
their

desire to flit quickly
branch
to bobbing branch

Being

unexpectedly awake this
dawn,

eaten too much, it's
times

like this I feel close to
whom-

ever I was, knowing
talk

is futile as my head
was

always cloud borne:
sub-

marine clouds and
sleeping

through last night's
fire-

ball's tattered flannel
as

I practice redressing
my

soul for a different
last

voyage, attempting to
keep

everything light for
rising

Sigh

if we had a large
enough
box we could attempt
sending
all those humming
birds
back to where ever
she
is resting now as
her
last years of a medical
Guinea
pig she was composed
in
a porcelain pose similar
to
her gifted birds that now
look
down from the nick-
nack
shelf and require
dusting
sighs in her name

On my 77th

words silent play were
to me
a pleasurable time
but
now it seems that I
wander
in a dry word-forest
devoid
of bear, fed birds

panting
now suffices for cog-
nition,
whatever that means,
yet
seems to keep me on
trail
of sighing dogs, colder
moon

Silence

I wanted to avoid this
Spring's
blistering greens

call it an old man's
chat,
a hydrogen line

frequency's
quiet
as I remain under,

irrelevant, slow milt of
scree-
one of the ones we

used
to glissade- evedince is
over-

whelming at this sub-
atomic
gamble as if my day

dreams determined the
amount
of covering rocks and
what

I'm going to do about
Its
Parallel erosions in the

library
of conscious, of spoken
words,

poems and the sudden
different
silence of a resting word

Mate

well my dear you
have
imagined your own
soul
as wispy cloud, vol-

uptuous
woman and well you
should
but mine I inherited
as

thinnest pencil with a
core
of a distant star
sent
to me by its light

as
I waited expectantly
to
draw fire in this peculiar
world

That's it

Star shine

has occluded
my
dreams of last night

Max- Ali
Ali- Max

bluebirds on their final
separate
journeys

Also
a good friend in my
youth

fighting a journeyman
who was just trying
to hang on himself

That's it we never
saw the blow that did it
just heard the bellending
the round

slid off the stool
turning bluebird

that's it we never see
a bad habit going past
the point: The Point

we follow the ambulance
eerie siren screams
hope in our ears

Often

in the olden
days
I memorized a
poem
on my way home
then
wrote on paper
typed
it on another and
swore
to myself that
I
had something sub-
stantial

now I print on
blank
screens that seem
to be
attached to my
computer's
nebulous hold on a
part
of the internet swirl-
ing
around the universe
on

a routed bus where
hand-less

net holders dip for
blips
of chance- of me-
to
dine upon

Ambulance

hooded and bloated
divided
in two, into
sneaking
back to my
city
of night-nay, answer
me- lying in
wait

twenty miles away
to
null infinity's
blank-
ness honed on the
event
horizon of tall
grey
buildings fed by

traffic
circles I plunge
into
down town's rifled
shots

Amazement

As foolish fish on
slippery
hook, clueless
what
has just happened

I see symbols not
images
while lithium
breaks
shattered in beryllium's

nuclei
particles, my mediator
between
normal and dark
matter

bangs generation
creeps
forward and only this
hook
allows me to stay

drifting
expanses expansion
seemingly
stable in and out of
light

Troubled

this has been a
long
walk for me in
my
condition that has
gone
from caged living
alone
loving trouble in a
single
dialectal monotone
to
the city of not being
anything

I felt as though I
stuck
my hand in a shark
jaw
painlessly after Mom
and
dad did not recognize
me
but smiled and waved

welcome
and I waved back as
we
passed closer than
possible

Easy target

melting neurons
stain of running
water on dreams

birds in a puddle
hypnotic repetitions
crenellations

in puddle's mirror
Let he who remembers
my face fly crowly

to my houses pitch
darkness that sticks
to this coming fog

it was early evening
when I slipped into
this dour fog horn

night gave chase
remember I can
still hear you3

From beyond the pale

That
this body's mere

shell

sown
liberally

DNA's

RNA's brought

Me

here
powered

by

a bag
of pebbled ice

solar

wind
blows and

my

head
croons with

light

and the
wonder is

head

bones
can house it

all

I
circle the bright
Circle

bewildered
in still-

ness,

in
rationalized coma,

un-

furling
leaves deserts

expect

being driven
on this

line

of lost
mindfulness

alone

www.ingramcontent.com/pod-product-compliance
Lightning Source LLC
LaVergne TN
LVHW041219080426
835508LV00011B/994